Milk & Cookies Press
Manhanset House
POB 342
Dering Harbor NY 11965
bricktower@aol.com ● www.ibooksinc.com

Cover design by Dean Motter
Interior design by Gilda Hannah
Edited by Howard Zimmerman
Front cover art by Joe Tucciarone
Back cover art by Christopher Srnka

Art Credits: Pages 1, 31 © 2002 Joe Tucciarone. Page 3 © 2002 James McKinnon.
Pages 4-5, 13, 17 © 2002 Phil Wilson. Page 6 © 2002 Patrick O'Brien. Pages 7-8 © 2002 Christopher Srnka.
Pages 9, 12 © 2002 John Sibbick. Pages 10, 27 © 2002 Dan Varner.
Page 11 © 2002 Alex Ebel. Page 12 © 2002 John Sibbick. Pages 14-15, 24-25, 28 © 2002 Douglas Henderson.
Pages 18, 19, 29 © 2002 Gregory S. Paul. Page 21 © 2002 Sharon Cox. Page 23 © 2002 Jan Sovak.

Library of Congress Cataloging-in-Publication Data

Olshevsky, George.
Tyrannosaurus Rex / by George Olshevsky and Sandy Fritz.
p.cm.—(Discovering dinosaurs)
1. JUVENILE NONFICTION / Animals / Dinosaurs & Prehistoric Creatures.
2. JUVENILE NONFICTION / History / Prehistoric.
3. JUVENILE NONFICTION / Animals / Reptiles & Amphibians.

ISBN 978-1-59687-750-4

First Milk & Cookies printing, December 2025

TYRANNOSAURUS REX

Sandy Fritz and George Olshevsky

MILK &
COOKIES
PRESS
™

Milk & Cookies Press
Habent Sua Fata Libelli

Dinosaurs lived on Earth from about 227 million to 65 million years ago. Scientists call this the Mesozoic era. It is also called the Age of Reptiles or the Age of Dinosaurs. Dinosaurs were closely related to today's reptiles and birds. In fact, many scientists now think that birds evolved from a small meat-eating dinosaur that was a swift runner. All dinosaurs were land animals. Flying reptiles (called pterosaurs) and reptiles that swam in the sea also lived during this period, but they were not dinosaurs.

The Age of Dinosaurs, the Mesozoic era, is divided into three periods. The earliest period is called the Triassic, which lasted from 248 million to 205 million years ago. Dinosaurs first appeared around the middle of this period. The Jurassic period followed, lasting from 205 million to 145 million years ago. The final period is called the Cretaceous. The Cretaceous spanned from 145 million to 65 million years ago. After the Cretaceous, dinosaurs were gone.

But during their time, dinosaurs lived everywhere on Earth, even in Antarctica. About 700 different kinds of dinosaurs have been unearthed, and many more remain in the ground awaiting discovery. There were meat-eating dinosaurs that could run fast on their long hind legs. There were four-legged, plant-eating dinosaurs 150 feet (46 m) long and weighing as much as 100 tons (91 t)! There were dinosaurs with horns, crests, and bony armor. Some dinosaurs, both meat-eaters and plant-eaters, were as small as chickens or house cats.

Everything we know about dinosaurs comes from fossils that people have dug up from the ground. Scientists examine, measure, and analyze these fossils. From them we can learn when and where dinosaurs lived. We have learned how dinosaurs walked and ran, what they hunted, and what plants they ate. We can even figure out how long they lived. Presented in this series is the most up-to-date information we have learned about dinosaurs. We hope you'll enjoy reading all about the fabulous beasts of Earth's distant past.

> *Tyrannosaurus rex* means "king tyrant lizard." A whole family of dinosaurs, called tyrannosaurids, was named after it. Other tyrannosaurids are *Tarbosaurus*, *Gorgosaurus*, *Albertosaurus*, and *Daspletosaurus*. They all looked similar to *T. rex*, but lived at different times in different parts of the world.

Tyrannosaurus Rex and Its World

Tyrannosaurus rex (*T. rex*) was a giant, meat-eating dinosaur that first appeared on Earth about 70 million years ago. It walked on its hind legs, with its long tail held straight out behind it for balance. It had small arms that ended in two clawed fingers. *Tyrannosaurus* had the smallest arms found on any meat-eating dinosaur, even though it was the largest meat-eating dinosaur ever to live in North America.

A large, fully grown *Tyrannosaurus* measured about 45 feet (14 m) from nose to tail—the length of an 18-wheeled tractor-trailer. It weighed up to six tons (5.5 t)—about as much as one large elephant. Its head was almost five feet (1.5 m) long, and it had incredibly powerful jaws filled with 58 huge teeth. Its mouth was so big it could have swallowed a person whole. It could rip off a 500-pound (230 kg) chunk of meat with a single bite.

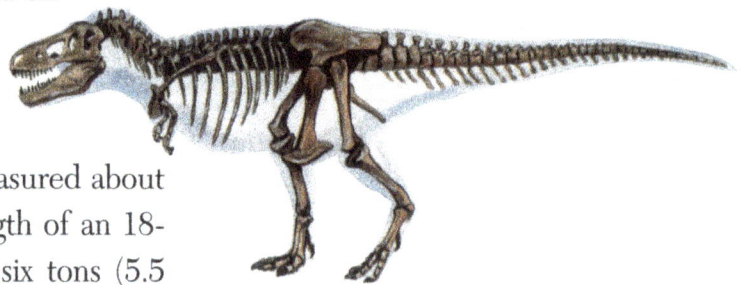

This page: The skeleton of a *T. rex*. Its skull was four to five feet (1.2–1.5 m) long. Opposite page: A *T. rex* surprises a *Parasaurolophus*, a "duck-billed" plant-eater.

Scientists date fossils by how old the layer of rock is where the fossilized bones are found. Most *Tyrannosaurus* fossils have been found in rock layers that were once river bottoms, swamps, or lakes, dating from the very end of the Age of Dinosaurs—about 70 million to 65 million years ago. But this does not mean *Tyrannosaurus* was a swamp dweller. Instead, flash floods may have swept the bones into rivers and swamps after the animals died.

Fossil parts from more than 30 different *Tyrannosaurus* skeletons have been discovered. Many consist of just a few bones and teeth, but a few *Tyrannosaurus* skeletons have been found that are almost complete. These fossils all have been found in western North America. They have been found as far north as Alberta and Saskatchewan in Canada, and as far south as Texas and New Mexico. Many scientists believe that *Tyrannosaurus* may have ranged as far north as the Arctic Circle and as far south as Mexico.

This page and opposite page: Tyrannosaurs did not live in swampy areas. However, they did hunt along streams and rivers, hoping to catch young plant-eaters while the dinosaurs were drinking.

Before the 20th century, scientists had no idea that a dinosaur like *Tyrannosaurus* ever existed. The great fossil collector Barnum Brown found the first *Tyrannosaurus* in Montana in 1902. Brown was sent out west to find fossils for the American Museum of Natural History in New York City. The museum's chief fossil scientist, Henry Fairfield Osborn, studied the fossils that Brown sent back. In 1905, Osborn published a report on the mysterious new animal, which he called *Tyrannosaurus rex*.

Osborn's report had an illustration of the *Tyrannosaurus* skeleton. Finally, scientists knew what *Tyrannosaurus* fossils looked like. They went hunting through unidentified bones in the basement of the American Museum of Natural History. Some were discovered to have belonged to *Tyrannosaurus*.

Opposite page: A *T. rex* feeds on the dead body of a *Triceratops*. This page: A *T. rex* is about to attack a young *Pentaceratops*. But it had better watch out for the horns!

What Tyrannosaurus Ate

Just what did a *Tyrannosaurus* eat? The short answer to this question is *anything it wanted*! A glance at the huge teeth of this dinosaur shows that it must have been a meat-eater. The real question is *what kind* of meat did it eat, which is a polite way of asking *who* did it eat. Most scientists believe it killed and ate other dinosaurs, and in particular, the many plant-eaters that lived in the same region. But some of these dinosaurs could have defended themselves quite well against a *Tyrannosaurus* attack. The three-horned *Triceratops* and the armored, tank-like *Ankylosaurus* were especially well prepared to fight back. Others, such as the "duck-billed" dinosaurs (*Edmontosaurus* and *Anatotitan*) and the dome-headed dinosaurs (*Stygimoloch* and *Pachycephalosaurus*), might have been able to outrun it. Like most large

Opposite page: A *T. rex* feeds on the body of a dead animal. This page: Two tyrannosaurs watch in frustration as an *Ornithomimus* runs past them. This bird-mimic dinosaur was a very fast runner.

predators today, including lions and hyenas, *Tyrannosaurus* probably hunted the young, sick, and weak plant-eating animals that were unable to put up a very good fight or to run away.

A harder question to answer is just how *Tyrannosaurus* hunted. Did it hunt alone, or in packs of two or more? Scientists look to the fossil record to try to figure out the answers. For example, in 1990, the largest, most complete *Tyrannosaurus* fossil yet discovered was dug up in South Dakota. She was nicknamed "Sue," after the person who found her. Fossil bones from three other *Tyrannosaurus* were found nearby. These three were smaller than Sue and were probably younger. Some scientists think that they might have been Sue's "family." The more such groups of *Tyrannosaurus* fossils we find, the more likely it seems that *Tyrannosaurus* lived in family groups or packs.

Scientists can also make guesses by looking at large predators living today. The largest land predators today are polar bears, which live isolated lives and come together only to mate. The same is true for tigers. Lions, however, live and hunt in packs, and so

An illustration of the *T. rex* nicknamed Sue as she might have looked in life.

do wolves. The largest reptilian predators—alligators, crocodiles, and Komodo dragons—live in large groups.

Although they may have lived in packs, the size of an adult *Tyrannosaurus* makes it unlikely that they hunted together. A full-grown, giant *Tyrannosaurus* probably would not have wanted to share its meal, even with other family members. But smaller, younger *Tyrannosaurus* may have hunted together. And they may have shared their kill.

Tyrannosaurus Junior

So far, no one has yet uncovered a *Tyrannosaurus* nest. Scientists must study other animals for clues about how *Tyrannosaurus* may have raised its young. The closest living relatives of dinosaurs are birds and reptiles. Both of these animals lay eggs, as did the dinosaurs. Birds sit on their nests while their babies grow inside the eggs. Their bodies keep the eggs warm until the babies are ready to come out. Some large reptiles, such as crocodiles, would crush their eggs if they sat on them. So crocodiles and alligators build nests over their eggs. They use dead plants to cover them. As the plants decay, they give off heat. This keeps the eggs warm. When the eggs are ready to hatch, the babies make faint cries, and the mother alligator helps them dig out of the nest. It is possible that large dinosaurs such as *Tyrannosaurus* hatched the same way.

A pack of tyrannosaurids tackles *Styracosaurus*, a horned plant-eater. This would have happened only if the plant-eater was sick, wounded, or very old. The scent of a dying animal would have brought predators from miles around.

After baby alligators hatch, their mother takes care of them for only a short while. She shows them where to find food and what to eat. When baby birds hatch, their mother stays with them for a longer time—until they can fly and are ready to leave the nest on their own. She finds food and brings it to the nest for them.

Tyrannosaurus young may have hatched like alligators, their eggs warmed under a mound of rotting plant matter. They may then have been taken care of like baby birds, having food brought to them in the nest.

Discoveries of fossils from *Tyrannosaurus* young show that the babies were slender and long-legged, with long, low heads. They probably started out by catching large insects and other small ani-

Opposite page: A mother tyrannosaur goes hunting with her half-grown offspring. Below: A juvenile *T. rex* tries to make a meal of baby pterosaurs. *Quetzalcoatlus* was the largest flying reptile that ever lived.

mals that lived in the underbrush. As they grew larger and stronger, they became able to catch larger animals such as lizards and, in time, small dinosaurs and baby dinosaurs.

Young tyrannosaurs were built for speed. This helped them chase down their next meal and run away from becoming one. As they grew, their bones became larger, and their jaws became deeper and more powerful. Studies of *Tyrannosaurus* bones show that the hatchlings grew fairly quickly. By about age seven they were already 20 to 25 feet (6–7 m) long, about half of their full adult size. These youngsters were capable of preying on all but the largest plant-eating dinosaurs. At that age, however, their heads were still rather long and low, and their jaws lacked the biting power of an adult.

A young *T. rex*, about half-grown, hunts small dinosaurs in the underbrush.

No one knows for sure how long it took *Tyrannosaurus* to grow to its full adult size, or even how big it could have grown. The largest *Tyrannosaurus* fossils found reflect an animal that measured about 45 feet (14 m) in length and weighed up to six tons (5.5 t). Other tyrannosaurids were usually smaller. Scientists think that tyrannosaurids continued growing for 30 years or more.

Even in adults, the forelimbs, or arms, of *Tyrannosaurus* were tiny, and the hands had only two clawed fingers. The arms were too small to meet each other across the chest. In other words, *Tyrannosaurus* couldn't even clap its hands. They were also too short to reach in front of the jaws, so they probably weren't used to hold something that *Tyrannosaurus* was biting or eating. Although they were small for a giant dinosaur, they were still about the same size as the arms of a grown man. And they were strong. Scientists have recently figured out that *Tyrannosaurus* might have been able to lift more than 400 pounds (182 kg) with each of those "puny" arms!

Tyrannosaurus may have used its forelimbs to help stand up after resting on its belly. Some scientists think that *Tyrannosaurus* would have been unable to get up from the ground without being able to brace itself with its forelimbs. But this is a tough theory to test, and we may never know for sure how *Tyrannosaurus* used its small but powerful arms.

Relatives of Tyrannosaurus

About 200 dinosaurs related to *Tyrannosaurus* are now known. They were meat-eating dinosaurs that walked and ran upright on just their hind legs; they had forelimbs that were not used in walking; and they kept their bodies balanced with their long tails. In 1881, scientist Othniel Charles Marsh called such dinosaurs "theropods," which comes from the

Tarbosaurus comes from the Greek word for "fearsome lizard." It was first reported in 1955 by the Russian scientist Yevgenii Alexandrovich Maleyev. He described a huge fossil skull. It was as large as any skull then known for *Tyrannosaurus*.

T. rex's arms were too short to be useful while hunting. How they were used remains a mystery.

Greek language and means "beast-foot." He called them this because they had four toes on each foot, like many mammals do today. But theropod feet look much more like the feet of modern birds than they do the feet of mammals. This is one of the reasons why many scientists think birds are living descendants of the theropods.

The family of theropods to which *Tyrannosaurus* belongs is called *Tyrannosauridae*, and the dinosaurs on this branch are called "tyrannosaurids." Henry Fairfield Osborn named them after their most famous family member, *Tyrannosaurus*. Besides *Tyrannosaurus*, there are now at least six other well-known tyrannosaurid family members. Many scientists think that the closest known relative of *Tyrannosaurus* is *Tarbosaurus*, a tyrannosaurid found in Mongolia.

Tyrannosaurus seems to have appeared out of nowhere in western North America toward the end of the Cretaceous period—about 70 million years ago. Besides North America, tyranno-

A *Tarbosaurus* makes a surprise attack on a plant-eating *Saurolophus*. It is one of the hadrosaurs, which are also known as the "duck-billed" dinosaurs.

saurid fossils have been found in only one other region on Earth: eastern Asia. Scientists are not sure where tyrannosaurids appeared first. In North America, there is a fossil record of tyrannosaurids similar to but older than *Tyrannosaurus*. This might indicate that they were the ancestors of *Tyrannosaurus*. Three of these were *Albertosaurus*, *Gorgosaurus*, and *Daspletosaurus*. *Albertosaurus* is named after the province of Alberta, Canada, where it was found. *Gorgosaurus* comes from the Greek meaning "Gorgon lizard." *Daspletosaurus* comes from the Greek meaning "frightful lizard." All three first appeared about 70 million years ago in western Canada and the United States. *Albertosaurus* and *Gorgosaurus* were about 25 feet (8 m) long as adults, while *Daspletosaurus* was about 30 feet (9 m) long, more powerfully built, with larger teeth. All three had bony ridges above their eyes, called brow horns. *Tyrannosaurus*, however, did not have these.

Scientists think that *Tyrannosaurus* may be more closely related to *Tarbosaurus*, an Asian tyrannosaurid. *Tarbosaurus* had a large head with a narrow snout, held horizontal to the ground. Its head was quite similar to those of *Albertosaurus*, *Gorgosaurus*, and *Daspletosaurus*, but like *Tyrannosaurus*, *Tarbosaurus* lacked brow

Tarbosaurus stalks the ancient Mongolian forests. *T. rex*'s Asian cousin may have been its closest relative.

horns. Its skeleton closely resembled the bones of the American tyrannosaurids.

About 85 million years ago, the world's sea level was much lower. Asia and North America were connected by a narrow stretch of land that is today covered by a strip of water called the Bering Strait. Tyrannosaurids must have migrated from one continent to the other on this land bridge. Asia is where the earliest and most primitive tyrannosaurids have been found. So most scientists believe that the tyrannosaurid family came from Asia and migrated to North America, rather than the other way around.

Alectrosaurus is the oldest, most primitive tyrannosaurid known. It lived around 95 million years ago in Mongolia. It was the same size as *Albertosaurus*, but more slender, with long legs. At first, the scientist who studied it thought it was only a distant relative of *Tyrannosaurus* because its front limbs, or arms, seemed much longer than those of other tyrannosaurids. Later research showed that the fossil arms had come from another kind of dinosaur, not *Alectrosaurus*. Its real arms were very similar to the arms of *Tyrannosaurus*.

A young *Daspletosaurus* chases down a meal. This early North American tyrannosaurid was smaller than *T. rex*. It weighed less, and probably could run much faster.

The Death of Tyrannosaurus

Sixty-five million years ago, a meteorite the size of a mountain crashed into the earth. The resulting explosion was the most powerful impact ever known to strike the planet. The crater left behind by the impact, found in Mexico, appears to have been more than 100 miles (160 km) across.

Worldwide fires were started by falling hot debris. Tidal waves a mile (.6 km) high flooded coastal areas. And a dark cloud of dust would have shrouded the world for many months or even years after the impact. The cloud was so thick that sunlight could not penetrate it. This killed many plants, which depend on sunlight to live. The death of the plants resulted in the death of the remaining plant-eating dinosaurs. And the death of the plant-eaters resulted in the death of the animals that fed on them—the meat-eating dinosaurs. Any dinosaurs not killed by falling rocks, fire, or tidal waves eventually died because their food vanished. This is what probably happened to *Tyrannosaurus*. Scientists are almost certain that *Tyrannosaurus* lived right up to the day of the impact.

An artist pictures *T. rex* at the time of the deadly meteor strike that killed off the dinosaurs and many other kinds of animals.

Many smaller species of animals, such as fish, frogs, turtles, birds, and crocodiles, did survive the asteroid impact. Another group of animals not only survived but prospered. Mammals quickly filled the gaps left behind by the dinosaurs and became the next group of animals to dominate the planet.

GLOSSARY

Albertosaurus (al-BURR-tuh-SAWR-us): a tyrannosaurid similar to *T. rex*, but slightly smaller.

Alectrosaurus (a-LEK-tro-SAWR-us): a tyrannosaurid. Same size as *Albertosaurus*, with longer, thinner legs.

Anatotitan (an-AT-oh-TIE-tan): a hadrosaurid dinosaur.

Ankylosaurus (an-KIE-luh-SAWR-us): largest of the ankylosaurs. It had an armored head and bony plates.

Daspletosaurus (das-PLEET-uh-SAWR-us): a tyrannosaurid dinosaur.

Edmontosaurus (ed-MON-tuh-SAWR-us): one of the largest of the hadrosaurs.

fossil (FAH-sill): a remnant of a living organism that has turned to stone over time.

fossilize (FAH-sill-eyez): the process by which organic remains are turned into stone.

Gallimimus (gal-ih-MY-mus): a large ostrich-shaped dinosaur with a long, stiff tail.

Gorgosaurus (GOR-guh-SAWR-us): a North American tyrannosaurid.

hadrosaurs (HAD-ruh-sawrz): the "duck-billed" dinosaurs.

Komodo dragon (ko-MOE-doe DRAG-in): one of the largest living reptilian predators.

Pachycephalosaurus (pak-ee-sef-AL-uh-SAWR-us): a plant-eating, "bone-head" dinosaur. It had a skull nearly 10 inches (26 cm) thick.

Parasaurolophus (PAR-uh-SAWR-uh-LOH-fus): a "duck-billed" plant-eater.

predator (PRED-uh-tor): an animal that hunts and eats other animals for food.

pterosaurs (TERR-uh-sawrz): flying reptiles from the Mesozoic era.

Quetzalcoatlus (KETZ-al-co-AHT-lus): the largest flying reptile to have ever lived.

Stygimoloch (stij-ih-MOL-uck): dome-headed dinosaur, with many spikes on its skull.

Styracosaurus (stih-RAK-uh-SAWR-us): a horned plant-eater.

Tarbosaurus (tahr-bow-SAWR-us): a tyrannosaurid. Similar to *T. rex* but more lightly built.

theropods (ther-UH-podz): group of two-legged meat-eaters that had birdlike qualities.

Triceratops (try-SER-uh-tops): a ceratopsid dinosaur with a three-horned face, powerful beaked jaws, and a short, bony frill.

Tyrannosauridae (tie-RAN-uh-SAWR-ih-day): the family of theropods to which the tyrannosaurs belong.

Tyrannosaurus rex (tie-RAN-uh-SAWR-us REX): a tyrannosaurid. One of the largest meat-eaters that ever lived.

www.ingramcontent.com/pod-product-compliance
Lightning Source LLC
Chambersburg PA
CBHW062333150426
42813CB00078B/2784